Also by Juliette van der Molen:

Death Library: The Exquisite Corpse Collection

Mother, May I?

Mother, May I?

Juliette van der Molen

ANIMAL HEART PRESS

It takes the heart of an animal

ISBN 978-0-359-44866-1

Library of Congress Control Number: 2019936409

Book design: Wijnand van der Giessen
Cover design: Amy Alexander

Printed in the United States of America

PUBLISHER

Animal Heart Press
Thetford Center, Vermont, 05075
Email: animalheartpress@gmail.com
Website: www.animalheartpress.net

Advance Praise

In the expertly explored territory of abuse and survival, Juliette van der Molen's *"Mother, May I?"* most certainly gives us something to cry about, but not in the way intended in the refrain that rolls through her work—instead we gather up the words of many desperately wounded children and women and weep with them. There is an extraordinary bravery in van der Molen's work, voices already in the midst of distress addressing newborn children, mothers who are no longer able to mother and become murderers. This is not a book for the faint of heart, but it is a book for those who know the constructs of motherhood have not served us well—and most certainly have not served our children. Though each poem is a deftly constructed wound, watch carefully for the tender detail, the brutally beautiful images that transport us from tragedy to a world of possibility.

Jen Rouse, author of *Riding with Anne Sexton*

Juliette van der Molen's *"Mother, May I?"* unveils a sense of recognition through experiencing motherhood while simultaneously mothering oneself. The pieces within this haunting collection speak to one another on being a mother, on being a daughter, on being. As readers, we witness a deconstructing of the patriarchy and, through this visceral reliving, can physically feel how painful looking back can be. We see assault and healing, we see a seeking of truth; we see the relearning of love—a correction of muscle memory. The language within dissects and reassigns meaning throughout. Above all else, there is an examination of the complexities of humans in the evolution of the roles we exist within. Nature meets nurture, humans vs. creatures— how they're one and the same. The plain incorruptibility and wildness that is childhood melding with the dissolving of traditional femininity. It is political in its questioning—an always-expanding resistance that rises and falls with the breath of each piece's speaker and paradigm. *"Mother, May I?"* is rich in pop culture and feminism, while holding tight to an honesty that strikes deep. It is a treasure of a collection that left me feeling both hungover and regenerated.

Savannah Slone, author of *Hearing the Underwater*

"Mother, May I?" is a chilling poetry anthology that evokes, in its author's note, an Institution of Motherhood. Imagine, dear reader, a constructed social expectation that motherhood is "martyrdom done right". Shades of red cloaks and white bonnets pass through our minds, and to be presented with motherhood as any kind of institution immediately sends alarm bells ringing. Thoughts of faceless figures, rules and horrific punishments for stepping out of line creep uncomfortably to the fore.

Juliette van der Molen is a truth-teller. "These are my truths," she says, for, like all of us, she is not multitudes. She is poet. One person. And yet… she can feel the weight of the Institution bearing down on her as she tries to forge her own path, acknowledging the child she once was and the mother she now is.

Mother, may i
explain to you
how i learned things
were my fault,
that i should know better

The opening poem sends chills running down the spine, and immediately sets the tone and spirit of the harsh lessons we all need to learn if we can give the mothers and children of past, present and future the room to breathe and be themselves, not just faceless figures following and fearing the commands of an invisible puppet master.

Mother, May I is such a charming phrase – on the surface, at least. So Downton Abbey; so Mary Poppins. There's no harm in it, surely? It's a simple cue of politeness that children may be taught in order to fit in. But, as the child requests permission of their mother to tell their own truth, each stanza reveals a new horror, a new link in the restrictive chain that parents and children feel tightening around their neck whenever they have an impulse to rail against the social institution that binds us all.

Mothers can harm children, and harmed children can grow up uncertain about how to bloom through damage done to them. Harmed children can grow up into mothers that harm children. The cycle repeats. The Institution has won.

But the Institution of Motherhood must not win. It must be seen, and seen clearly, through the eyes of brave, bold, beautiful poets like Juliette van der Molen who yearn to rip society's chains from their neck so they can breathe again. Juliette van der Molen's anthology is a gift – the gift of clarity, and wisdom, and understanding, and freedom. It offers us a chance to see beyond the cloaks and bonnets to the faces beneath. The Institution of Motherhood depends on us not being able to see that it exists. It depends on us believing in it without question. Juliette's voice is a roar, a beacon of light, that shows us the tattered state and cobwebbed corners of the Institution, and shatters its effigies into a million tiny pieces.

This book is important. You do not need to be a mother to read this book. It is enough that you have once been a child. Follow your heart, walk your own path, and smash the Institution. It is brittle, and its time is done. You must have your freedom to grow.

I shall leave the final words to Juliette van der Molen:

"The narrative of the Institution of Motherhood can never be changed until we start telling the truth."

Magda Knight, Founding Editor of Mookychick

For the children

Author's Note

Motherhood is cloaked and often smothered by the man made institution surrounding it. This may seem like semantics. However, to call this terminology semantics would be to oversimplify an important distinction. No one knew that better than Adrienne Rich. She reveals the truth of this in her essay, *Of Woman Born, Motherhood as Experience and Institution*, explaining how the institution of motherhood attempts to override a woman's personhood. As a feminist, I focus on forging new narratives that will affect future generations of women. What Rich taught me is that sometimes the narrative of the past runs so deep it is easy to forget where it came from and why it is so damaging. I always thought that ideas about motherhood came from the women before me. That's what I expected to find during my excavation into this body of work. What I found surprised me. These attitudes that want to force a morality of standards on a woman's behavior and place in society have but one beginning: the patriarchy.

Mothering was something that happened to me as a consequence of circumstance and expectations. My internal struggle between who I feel I am and who society expects me to be has been bitter. The institution that is motherhood presents us with Hallmark cards and breakfasts in bed. These were supposed to be the extensions of fairy tales beyond the happy ever after from my girlhood. The ideal mother is presented as a Madonna of sweet smiles covering up sacrifices for the greater good. Her entire identity becomes that of 'mother' with all other personal ambition set aside for the furtherance of the species. Motherhood is martyrdom done right.

Except this isn't the truth most women live. For mothers like me, these expectations have left a wake of damage that I'm only beginning to undo.

This book uncovers a different side of motherhood. Some of this poetry is based on my own history as a daughter while others are sentiments from myself as a mother. Folded into this are many horrific and heinous acts that some mothers visit on their children. These are acts that, regardless of gender, we struggle to understand. There is damage here. These are the terrors that make women feel that they must do anything to not be *that* mother. At all costs, they must not be the permissive Kitty Menendez, the incestuous Anne Sexton, the vain Joan Crawford or even that mother next door who yells loudly enough for the neighbors to hear. These poems do not seek to forgive or make excuses for any of these transgressions. They are here to illuminate that the experience of motherhood is sometimes devastating to all involved.

Children are the ultimate victims in each one of these cases. Some of them have their lives taken by the one person who is supposed to love them unconditionally and protect them from the world. Still others are so changed and devastated by the impact of abuse that it affects them long into their adult lives. They are riddled with pain that never fully heals. The narrative of the institution of motherhood can never be changed until we start observing reality and telling the truth.

These are my observations. These are my truths.

Juliette van der Molen

Content Warning

The poems in this collection touch on many difficult subjects.

There are poems that contain elements of struggles with mental health, child abuse, filicide and suicide. If you choose to read this collection, it may be important to exercise self-care and take breaks where necessary.

Contents

Mother, May I?

Mother, May I?

Mother, may i
ask you why
it was so different
to be first born?
did i alter you
to this
stretched
&
unreal smile
or were you always
unhappy
&
birthed me
that way?

Mother, may i
go back in time
and do things
different, maybe
smaller
&
less vocal,
a whisper that
would say
'yes please'
&
'no thank you'
to save
tender insides
where my cheeks
bleed against teeth?

Mother, may i
explain to you
how i learned things
were my fault,

that i should know better,
that pain was a
consequence
&
punishment
so deserved?
did you know that
when he
hit me
&
his mouth opened
your voice
shrilled against
my enamel—
look what you
made me do!

Mother, may i
distance myself
across state lines
&
oceans where
you can cross
only occasionally
to remind me
of how things
were
&
weren't,
this kaleidoscope
of jammed memories
that must be real,
because you say so.

Mother, may i
remind you that
i didn't choose to be
your daughter

&
your albatross,
nor did i want to
be noticed so much
by your
hands
&
wooden spoons.

Mother, may i
have some
peace
&
quiet,
the kind that you always
yelled
&
begged for,
even when i tried to be
so small.

Cookie Cutter

These are the memories
meant to be sweet,
Christmastime treats—
a batter stirred,
simple choices,
a dough kneaded light
to keep it tender,
rolled thin,
ready to cut shapes—
trees & stars,
bells & wreaths,
mother's rolling pin
setting a course for tradition.
cookies cut and sugared right—
'trees are green, not red!',
she says and i learn
to wallpaper an obedient face.
my hands fist into my
Raggedy-Ann printed apron,
wrinkling ruffled trim,
knees pressed in silent
prayer against a wooden
seat that won't forgive me,
hard just like the smile
that she turns on me,
a mouth that opens
and threatens to eat
my thoughts alive
no matter how silent they are.
so—
i sugar all the trees green,
and wait for the falling
hand of justice
she hovers over my head.

Six Little Letters

the power
of six little letters
is more than i can
bear.
i jumble them in
my mind
so i don't have
to see them
all
at
once.
but they sit and wait,
they know that i know,
one day they're coming
together and i won't
be able to hide anymore—

A little girl
  Before she's grown
    Underneath a watchful eye
      Sure that she's deserving
        Every time the hands that hurt her
          Deliver a lesson.

M(other)

her whistle from
inside the nest
alerts me—
where she stands,
watching (waiting),
for mistakes
&
bad behavior—
(bloodshot) eyes
veiled by glaring
summer sunshine
behind a screen meant
to keep out annoyances (me).
"don't you make me come out there!"
she declares when
i pick the strawberries
we (tried) to grow together
&
spirit them with me
hiding high
up in trees where
she can't see.
i hear
her hands plunged in
dirty dish water,
splashes
&
clatters
(angry) pottery against Formica,
my m(other),
(not) my heroine.

No seatbelt required

i used to love to ride in
your little bug, grey with
the neon orange pin stripes
that dad put on by hand,
making sure it was all straight,
going over every little
detail, until it was just right.

he wasn't there that day,
the day we ditched my
radio flyer and climbed inside,
my red gold curls bouncing
like a Shirley Temple doll—
hold on tight. i can't wait
to get to the Ben Franklin
and spend my dime on a
striped candy stick.

i try to think about this
instead of about how your
voice scratches against the
windshield, and you're all mad
but i don't know why. i've done
something i still can't remember,
but i'm pretty sure this means—
no candy this time.

i shrink against the door, in
the front seat,
before we ever knew about
safety and seat belts. i shut my
eyes tight because i still think
maybe i'll disappear while
you mangle the gears,
take the turn too fast and wide.

a slipped lever, no safety lock,
my luck is just right,
launched into a summer sun,
my sister wailing in the backseat,
gravel kissing my cheek, not you—
kneeling distraught by the side
of the road, i won't remember
this, but you will.

it's a raucous tale, hilarity
unfolded, your arms sweep
wide to make a big point—
the grand gesture. your eyes
wide 'i was terrified', while i
just push my potatoes around
the plate. i was trouble, always
trouble, worrying you and
making you weep. for a moment
while everyone laughs, i think
about my little body sailing
in the sunshine, about how i
was almost freed.

that's my secret to keep.

The Wait

waiting in the window
for the lights
that beam a path
of hope into the driveway.
a blue station wagon
from cross-country trips
and my brother crunched
in the middle between sisters
with longer legs,
traveling half the country
with the king of the road
and a half empty threat
i
will
pull
this
car
over
if the bickering doesn't stop.

waiting for dad to get home
to hear what i've done this time
and take care of business,
my comeuppance glowing red
on pale freckled cheeks
from the shrill smack
that caved me in on myself
until i crumpled
but held the tears at bay,
gave
me
something
to
cry
about
a gift i want to return,

but can't—
not yet.

waiting to hear his heavy boots
smacking the snow off in the entryway,
his feet throbbing a shift work song.
i'm the last thing he wants to deal with—
she
always
says,
but his discipline is slow and teaching,
with words meant to love me
rumbling low from a bowed head.

waiting to sit next to him on the edge
of the bed, while we talk about what happens
when mother's face turns red.
i
should
know
better,
i should be more like my sister—
he never says this,
but i know it's true.

waiting for him to say,
'this hurts me more than it hurts you',
his disappointment slamming hard in my heart,
when i want to say all the words—
every
last
syllable i own,
but i can't because i'm just a child
and mothers, they're not monsters,
they're cuddles and hugs, the weaker sex.
but softer hands clutch venomous words
lashed cruelly out with wet towel snaps,
delivered on a back or thigh with precise justice

and banishments to the beyonds.

waiting & waiting
for it all not to be true,
waiting & waiting
at
the
window
until the sun is gone.

What you call Love

this river of words
fraught with undertow
that drowns & fills
lungs already suffocated,
inhaling the vapor
of what you call love.
before you ever
laid hand to body:
cheeks,
buttocks
&
slender thighs,
i lost pieces
of my heart by the spoonful.
you—
slurping in secret,
taking your fill,
then tucking me in with smiles.

Now You See Me

naked huddled limbs pressed
to the water tap,
naughty children
just being children,
splashing water from
tub to floor.
until your roar reverberates
against tiles
& your face,
red blooded blush,
wooden spoon brandished
from a trembling hand
(is it anger or anticipation?)
ready for slick skin,
(mine)
ripe for marking.
i cover my sister,
as if she were in danger,
(though you & I know the truth)
in silent tears.
she cries openly, unaccustomed
to this fear because she is
well behaved & good,
unlike me—
this time my eyes squinch
up tight, closed so you
can't see me,
(except, you always can)
while you laugh,
unable to strike this time—
this is the story you'll tell
around a family dinner table,
saved special for holidays
or other occasions where
my sense of humor is not enough
to take the sting away.

Backtalk

too smart for your own good
//she says//

i don't like your tone
//she warns//

defiant teenage eye rolls
//she scowls//

hand lifted too quick to guard against
//she smacks//

fingerprints painting scarlet on a pale skinned cheek
//she screams//

don't talk back to me.

Dear Christina[1]

an eight year old's
pen pal letters
trading horse pictures
from New Zealand
for Smurf shrinky dinks
i baked with mother.

i saw you in a movie
and i thought,
we could have been
friends, Christina.
i would have given
up my exotic Colleen
in a second.

you were awkward,
gangly,
just like i always felt—
an interloper not belonging,
but always trying.

my shrinky dinks are
cooling, and i see
you on a television
that feels so far away.
your mother screams
of hangers and crushes
ice into her face.

my mother whispers low
into my ear,
'see what bad mothers do',
as if she's never hit me
or screamed like her heart

---

1   Christina Crawford suffered at the hands of her abusive and alcoholic adoptive mother, Joan
      Crawford.

came unglued.

i just nod and watch you cry,
i wish i could wipe
all of your tears
and maybe you'd wipe mine.
i see you grow fast,
in two hours' time,
you grow brave,
i wonder how to be like
you, and i want to clap
my hands.

mother scowls and shakes
her head when you talk back,
both yours
& mine,
a matching set.
you say mommie dearest,
i say 'i love you more'—
but neither of us means it,
we're marking time,
making sure.

i wrote you letters in
a journal, but never used
your name,
i wonder,
did you do the same?
when mother found them
her mouth opened
and out came
that shaking sound,
full of o's and s's
frosted a thick layer
of shame,
writing lies,
that could never be true,

how could they be when
mommie says she loves you?

i'm supposed to love you

i'm supposed to love you,
but my legs are thin under
the white hospital sheet,
and a belly i thought would
magically suck navel to spine
once more is a deflated sponge.
there are no cheers for me,
just quiet visits and hellos,
everyone's happy that you
are well— ten fingers,
all your toes. i still can't
make sense of you, outside
of me. eyes so wide beneath
a knitted cap they threaten
to swallow me whole. i
want to say i'm sorry now
because i don't know, how
to be this thing— called
mother. my girlhood left
me, pushed it all out
with you, struggled until
my hands shook and molecules
quaked. i'm supposed to love
you, but i'm not sure how.
why all these tears?
does it happen like magic?
is that how it goes?
if so, i'm already
failing, and this will be a surprise
to no one.

A Nightjar[2] has no Nest

our eggs shake with
the leaves down
in the loam where predators
roam, and where is our mother?
the wanderer
the nightjar—
prowling nocturnal,
leaves us nest-less
beneath a Hunter's Moon.
if she returns before
we are taken,
to spirit us away in
the confines of her beak
she might crack delicate
shells, because not all of nature
is meant to nurture.
our yolks run down
her gullet until she is bred again,
another chance to
leave birdlings nest-less
a cycle repeated
again
&
again,
under view of another
mother moon shaking in
the sky at her carelessness.

---

2   A nightjar is a nocturnal bird that usually builds her nest on the ground.

Mother Bear

we are still wet,
matted fur,
pushed sticky from
a womb,
our first hibernation.
before we turn
to suckle teat,
there is another
coming and you,
large paws and growls
have gnashed your
teeth into the firstborn
for no apparent reason.
the watchers, those
people things— they
call you monster bear,
though some take notes,
science & nature
still steeped
in mystic questions.

they say mother knows best
and maybe you do,
a body invaded,
connected bloodstream,
heartbeats syncopated
into morse code
only we understand.
they still call you
monster bear— but leave
what remains,
just two of us now,
cautious as you lick
and groom. when the
dust settles and all
is calm, you devour the

second and i am left
hiding my weakness, your
one and only.

taken, by human hands,
hairless coddled,
i am weak,
not fit to roam
mountain or zoo.
nourished from a man-made
nipple, i never
grow strong enough
and now they, who called
you monster— look with
curious wonder. because
you're just an animal,
nothing but instinct.
still, mother bear,
you knew.

Shoe Box Grave

trusted cradle hands
meant for tender heads
and lullaby sleeps,
meant to usher this
tabula rasa innocence
into the waiting arms
of the man in the moon—
digs a shoe box grave,
six feet deep.

she rests,
a bird with wings
folded inward,
feathers battered
by a wind too strong
that pushed her from
the nest, where she
should have been,
never was
(but should have been)
safe.

curled inside with less
care than a pair
of Jimmy Choo boots,
that once saw this
cardboard home,
she is skin and bones
without breath—
just blue lips
and a cry stilled,
colic, they said.

under the tree,
nestled near roots
in the backyard

of the house they sold
with the warm brown sugar
smell of chocolate chips
melted in an oven,
9 minutes,
not 9 months,
but devoured just as quickly.

took the first offer,
picked each room clean,
no need for baby shoes
she can't outgrow,
dropped in a box
marked salvation
for another baby,
more fortunate maybe,
with a mother less
likely to break.

3 A.M.

Doors fly open
along with the coat
of a mother,
baby crushed to her
chest—
my baby! she says,
though it's larger
than a baby, it's just
as small, fragile.
nothing good comes
at 3 A.M.,
nothing good comes
in Emergency.
Death number five,
her lips bunched blue
they're falling like
dominoes clicked together
with a mother's quick flick,
a death gene whispered
through the upstate trees,
nine little lives
birthed into Marybeth's[3]
arms and lullaby hands
offering smothered sleep
in cradles turned coffins.

---

3   Marybeth Tinning was convicted in 1985 of murdering her 4 month old daughter. She is suspected of
     killing her other children, but was never convicted. She was granted parole in July 2018.

Accomplice

it turns out that no amount of money
can save anyone from cruelty,
and in fact,
perhaps it becomes easier
to hide, something sinister
and expected below the middle
class upbringing where Kitty[4]
learned how wives & husbands—
mothers & fathers
knit a family together.

escaped to a Beverly Hills Mansion
where the walls are thicker,
but not thick enough
to shut out violence that happens
a room or two away,
and her son is screaming
(no, Erik, she won't save you)
for help until his cries are
muffled and mortified beneath
the heft and breath of
an executive who no one
could believe is such a capable monster.

so she'll pour another drink,
lift her feet onto the couch,
never thinking about what the
pain & suffering must feel like,
never considering how her child
knows she can hear, but turns her
ear from the wall, to press the
remote on the television.

---

4   Mary Louise 'Kitty' Menendez and her husband, Jose Enrique Menendez were murdered by their
     sons Erik and Lyle on August 20, 1989. The brothers alleged sexual abuse by their father. According
     to her sons, Kitty would turn up the television in order not to hear them being abused by their father.

he'll listen to the volume rise
(no, Lyle, she's not coming)
until he's nothing under the
hands of a father,
sinking despair into the
inaction of a mother,
cries for help useless,
battered relentless in
the most beautiful circumstances,
a child crying "mother why",
brothers banded together—
knowing that relief will only come
down the barrel of a shotgun
on the day that they die.

Mirror, Mirror

fairy tales are full of awful mothers,
some of them not quite mothers,
step-mothers far removed
from dead mothers who were
much better, saintly even—
pure of heart, if only
they had lived.

jealous of attention
paid by others, always
searching for adoration,
never realizing a daughter
might give it, sing songs
of love and praise from
ruby red lips, pull the
heart from her maiden breast
if only to please a mother
like the one she'd lost,
the only one she'd ever known.

just another female,
companion turned competition
for the folly of men. banished
to a forest, screaming through
the trees with a dress torn
to shreds. on the run from
a huntsman who can't bear
to kill, won't bend to the will—
who is somehow more
forgiving than the so-called
softer sex.

poisoned in a last ditch
effort, for the mirror on the
wall tells the tale of someone
fairer, the fairest of them all.

slipped under glass,
still beautiful,
protected by little men
(always! men!)
until another comes along,
his kiss proffered
to lift and claim her
into life again.

this is the story,
(oh! happy! ever! after!)
that little girls remember when
dreaming of a patriarchal rescue—
the only way to save them
from a mother's bitter end.

Something went very wrong that Night
for Michael and Alex[5]

it's been twenty years since
they were lost to everyone
& she, lost to herself amidst
conjecture so close to true,
though, not quite. she keeps
things close, guarding negatives
because exposing film to light
inflames.

something went very wrong when
she pressed kisses on their
foreheads, her fingers brushing
& fussing over tiny shoes,
so small, she could hide
them in her hand, pink feet
still warm & alive.

something went very wrong when
they reached arms out, not quite
long or strong enough, as she secured
& pulled seat belts meant for
safety. aching to be held,
they fuss, but this is the only
way she knows how to hold them
now, ignoring cries.

she was not herself, but she won't
say who she was. not the mother
& protector they needed,
deserved just by virtue of
breathing through helpless
mouths & flailing limbs.

---

5   Michael Daniel Smith (3 years old) and Alexander Tyler Smith (14 months old) were drowned when
     their mother, Susan Smith, strapped the children into her car and pushed it into a lake in 1994.

something went very wrong when
they opened mouths, because that's
what babies do, alerting
& telling mothers that things
aren't right. did they know
what she did while water filled
lungs, when they witnessed
a mother's betrayal?

she was not herself, this no one
will believe because the other
story is so much better, the
one where dirty laundry flaps
on a line. babies so innocent
& how could they not be? she
told a lie to save herself,
because it was easier, afforded
belief by the virtue of her
skin against that of an unknown
black assailant. wrapped herself
in a pure sheet of white
privilege.

it's been twenty years since
she heard tires crunching gravel
& rolled up the windows to
drown out screams. when asked
why, there is silence—
& speculation, she still won't explain,
just hellish repetition, damnable defense—
'i was not myself,' not in this story,
where 'something—
went very wrong that Night.'

Glamour Girl

not the first runner up, my baby's the glitz queen—
one of a kind in a custom made cupcake,
stones and frilly frosting above pristine knees.
oh, honey those hands better not move,
elbows straight please,
as you put those pretty feet in your model T.
she's got a college fund of tiaras,
a real winner, my girl.
if she doesn't nail this walk,
she better run like hell.
my pageant days are over,
now i have hers.
sometimes she gives me trouble,
nothing a whipping won't cure.
she wants stupid little things,
friends and candy bars.
but calories count,
and other girls— just competition.
she'll thank me when she ages out—
c'mon and give us a smile, princess,
before i give you something to cry about.

Megan's[6] Lullaby

months blurred by meth
and the clicking of teeth,
picking of skin,
stretching— under cover,
swelling seed,
she didn't do it on her
own, even though
she's alone
once again.

body turned currency,
loan sharked, never loved,
a desperation,
so predictable that
she won't even need
two lines to tell her
it's happened
once again.

this new normal,
this routine hums
as easily as rhymes
to fill an empty nursery
slips into sequence
once again.

do you reckon she
doesn't cry when
forever blue eyes
flutter closed and
breathing stops cold,
once again?

---

6   Megan Huntsman was convicted of murdering six of her children, all newborns, and storing them in
     boxes her her garage. She gave birth to all of these children between 1996 and 2006 and killed them
     by means of strangulation or suffocation immediately after birth. The babies were discovered when
     she left them behind after moving. Megan pled guilty to all charges.

do you think she'd do
anything else if she knew
how? but all she knows
is how to nestle
babies in a box,
singing a silent lullaby
to say goodbye
once again.

Linda's[7] lament

held beneath verse, sprinkled
in subtext like a secret seasoning
as she works her magic words
like kitchen witchery
gone to bedlam and back.

a mother holding nothing sacrosanct,
words spilled confessional to priestly page.
stopped short of contrition,
not seeking forgiveness,
communion wafer waived.

lauded feminist, prized poet and
a mother besides. little linda's crying
but no one seems to mind. sacrificed
to art, her own words stunted, changed.
a mother's kisses, meant to balm,
overwhelms, strips her instead.

a voice from the grave, no mercy[8] this—
just burdens a daughter bears
and braves to show the world.
grim glamour, a quiet slip into darkness;
cuddled in fur she's drenched in vodka,
one last peaceful narcissistic sleep.

.suicide complete.

---

7   Linda Gray Sexton, daughter of the poet Anne Sexton, was sexually abused by her mother. Dr.
      Michael Orne, psychaitrist, released tapes of therapy sessions with Anne to author Diane Wood
      Middlebrook. These tapes contain confessions of the sexual abuse she committed against her
      daughter.

8   During the years that Anne Sexton was sexually abusing her daughter, she was in the process of
      writing a play about a daughter's sexual abuse by a father and aunt. This play 'Mercy Street' was
      produced off Broadway in 1969.

A life stalled

for baby boy Drexler[9]

clandestine birth, yet
you were perfect, not
still, air slipped into
tiny lungs, i wonder
did you cry? if a baby cries
and
no one hears it,
is it still alive?

ten fingers, ten toes,
all the things a mother
hopes for, except,
maybe not yours. this—
the ultimate DIY.

when she chose her
dress she didn't know
it would be that night—
it's not a thing you
plan, baby boy, a
birth between dances,
alone,
in a stall,
while your boyfriend
waits for you.

where there is blood,
there is trauma. though all
we get are newspaper
facts, cold-hearted truths
on a page. no matter her

---

9   On June 6, 1997 Melissa Drexler gave birth to her son in a bathroom stall at her high school prom in
     New Jersey. She strangled the baby and suffocated him in a plastic bag before placing it in the
     garbage and returning to share a dance with her boyfriend. She was sentenced to 15 years in prison,
     but was paroled after serving 37 months.

excuse, she is damned
and you are dead. did
you both cry in and
out of this world until
it bounced from stall
to stall to a paper towel
dispenser that cannot
hold enough to staunch
the tragedy.

Beneath the Rubble

i am dust covered in the rubble, waiting
for the air to clear. and we are unearthing
this disaster piece by piece, hundreds of
rocks and other unearthly debris crowding
my field of vision:

a Christmas tree, chucked out
through a frosted front door,
in the snow,
ornaments broken and weeping wet.

strings cut on an instrument,
a gift from my father,
bridge smashed to oblivion
even though the sound post
stands strong, hidden inside.

ropes of scars over skin,
not the kind from
rites of passage,
like a childhood accident or birth.
the kind that shouldn't be there,
not accidental.

i clear these
one
by
one
and though I shake the dust
from my hair, it still clings
to every pore in my skin.
this coughing won't stop,
a disease that wants to be terminal.
i unearth a foundation,
after i thought the trauma cleared,
only to find your face

pressed in the mortar,
brows drawn together in the frown
that shows me why the bricks
came tumbling down in
the first place.

i need new tools, the kind i've
never held before and i think
of those three little pigs
you once told me about—
i start chipping you away then
until i build my own house
brick
by
brick
while you pace around my silence,
denied the power you once had, so
huff, mother, huff
and
puff, mother, puff
you're not the big bad wolf anymore.

Truth Serum

i know what you did
&
i'm saying it out loud,
because in my Midwestern way
i've covered for you
&
said nothing happened
that didn't happen
in any other house.

you know that's not true—
don't you?

i know what you did
when you told everyone
i was difficult,
a backtalker— moody.
you were laying groundwork
for them
&
me.

you know that's not true—
don't you?

i know what you did
when you were president
of the PTA for all those years,
baking cookies— leading troops
&
convincing everyone how sweet
you could be.

you know that's not true—
don't you?

i know what you did
when you thumbed your dirty
fingers through my diary,
looking for reasons— damning me
&
telling me it was wrong to
write these things.

you know that's not true—
don't you?

i know what you did
when you pushed me forward
as an example, of what not to do,
smiling— begging for sympathy
&
saying you tried to understand me.

you know that's not true—
don't you?

i know what you did
when you recalibrated memories,
fabricating details,
crowning yourself— a martyr
&
telling everyone you were
happy to sacrifice, for me.

you know that's not true—
don't you?

i know what you did
when you tried to tell me
i was just like you,
said we're friends— thick as thieves
&
best friends if i wanted to

just be agreeable like you.

you know that's not true—
don't you?

i know what you did,
how it cut so deep
that it shocked me
into silence
&
denial, until this reckoning
years in the making.

i know what's true—
&
i don't care if you do.

sorry

i wonder if i was sorry before
i was ever born. i took your
childhood & stole it for my own,
but mother, i'm so sorry.

i wonder if i learned this word
first, before i could speak it aloud
as you tumbled into another
pregnancy, trapped with us at home,
and mother, i'm so sorry.

i know this is my litany, for every
word i shouldn't have said, every
attitude i gave you, every time i
fled to slam my door & shake walls,
believe me mother, i'm so sorry.

i know this word replaces tears
that i learned not to shed, no
drama here that met with scorn
& always made you so mad,
oh mother, i'm so sorry.

i learned to say it for little things,
that meant nothing. for things
like pillows tilted askew &
the ice clinked in my glass,
because it hurt your head,
mother really, i'm so sorry.

i learned to use it like connective
tissue, a transition from my thoughts
to the man above me, lorded over
me. perhaps i could have been a
better wife, a better mother,
i promise mother, i'm so sorry.

i became all my 'sorries', pathetic
worn thin, the warp and weft of
me too porous to keep it in. so
when he said 'you're a sorry excuse
for a woman' i knew it was true,
just like mother said, i'm so sorry.

About the Author

Juliette van der Molen is a writer and poet living in the Greater NYC area. She is an intersectional feminist and a member of the LGBTQIA community.

Her work has also appeared in Burning House Press, Memoir Mixtapes, Collective Unrest and several other publications.

She is the author of the chapbook, Death Library: The Exquisite Corpse Collection (*Moonchild Magazine, 2018*) and the forthcoming Anatomy of a Dress (*The Hedgehog Poetry Press, November 2019*).

You can connect with her through Twitter via @j_vandermolen and www.JulietteWrites.com

Acknowledgments

A book never makes it into this state without support and help along the way. I'd like to thank Wijnand, for his love, dedication and work with book design to help bring this project to life. An early champion of my writing, he lifts me up when I am unsure and reminds me every day that what I have to say is valuable and important. Even though we are far apart, he has held me close through some of the most difficult parts of this process.

Additionally, I'm grateful for the passion and support of Animal Heart Press Editor in Chief, Elisabeth Horan, who helped spur my writing on with encouragement and kindness. Always an example of strength, she has given me motivation to push ahead when the going got rough. I am thrilled to be part of her new press and look forward to sharing in this publication adventure with her. Additional thanks to assistant editor Amanda McLeod who jumped on board to assist with promotional aspects of the book. I thank you for your strong spirit and creative energy.

Publications

Mother, May I? and *Shoe Box Grave* were published in *Anti-Heroin Chic*, November 2018.

Cookie Cutter was published in *Anti-Heroin Chic,* December 2018.

Beneath the Rubble was published in *The Hellebore,* December 2018.

i'm supposed to love you was published in *Kissing Dynamite,* February 2019.

Made in the USA
Las Vegas, NV
19 May 2021

23315477R00042